25 Lessons Learned From My Dog *Morgan*

By Sherry Davis, Ed.D.

Xulon
PRESS

Copyright © 2008 by Sherry Davis, Ed.D.

25 Lessons Learned From My Dog Morgan
by Sherry Davis, Ed.D.

Printed in the United States of America

ISBN 978-1-60647-403-7

All rights reserved solely by the author. The author guarantees all contents are original and do not infringe upon the legal rights of any other person or work. No part of this book may be reproduced in any form without the permission of the author. The views expressed in this book are not necessarily those of the publisher.

Unless otherwise indicated, Bible quotations are taken from The New King James Version, Copyright © 1982 by Thomas Nelson, Inc., and The Holy Bible, New International Version, Copyright © 1973, 1978, 1984 by the International Bible Society.

www.xulonpress.com

Table of Contents

1. Joy 11
2. Wherever He Leads 13
3. Helpless and Dependent 15
4. The Crate - a Holding Place 17
5. Being Stubborn 19
6. Love 21
7. His Efforts to Please Me 23
8. Being Inconvenienced 25
9. The Watchful Eye 29
10. Never Alone 31
11. The Big Mess 33
12. Being A Parent 37
13. Comfort During Painful Times 39
14. Staying Close to the Master 41
15. The Price of Disobedience 43

16. Labels 45
17. Giving the Best 49
18. The Restful Trip 51
19. Worms 53
20. Patience 55
21. My Delight 57
22. Promises to be Kept 59
23. Permission to Come Near 61
24. The High Price 63
25. Longing for the Master's Return 65

Acknowledgements

I am most grateful to God for my gift, my little dog Morgan. It is through my relationship with him that I've become more aware of your unending love for me. Heavenly Father, may this little book bring You glory and honor.

I appreciate my husband, Kyle, for his wonderful support. A special thanks to my twin sister, Terry, and her husband Ken for encouraging me along the way. Thanks to all of you for believing in me!

Introduction

25 Lessons Learned from My Dog Morgan is a little book that shares enlightening lessons learned from my little puppy, Morgan. Only after having him for about two months, the LORD began to flood my mind with a fresh awareness of the magnitude of His love. It is my pleasure to share my wonderful experiences with you!

1. Joy

These things I have spoken to you that My joy may remain in you, and that your joy may be full.
(John 15:11 NKJV)

I have wanted a dog for many years, but was unable to get one for different reasons. Finally, there came a point in my life that I could actually take care of a dog, so my husband and I decided to purchase an eight week old Bichon Frise. We decided to name him Morgan. He has a lot of personality and draws much attention because he loves everybody! It gives me much pleasure to see the smiles that Morgan brings to so many people. I've come to realize that my gift was not only for me – but he was also to be shared with others.

We have only had Morgan a little over three months and it's hard to imagine being without him. God gave me Morgan at a time when He knew I really needed him. God wanted me to experience joy in my life, which I had not experienced in a long time.

Prayer: Dear God, thank you for my precious gift, Morgan, and the joy he brings me as well as others. In Jesus' name, amen.

2. Wherever He Leads

…"Whoever desires to come after Me, let him deny himself, and take up his cross, and follow Me."
(Mark 8:34 NKJV)

Morgan and I have gotten very attached to each other, one reason is that I'm with him most of the day. What I've begun to notice is that Morgan follows me all around the house, from bedroom to bathroom to kitchen. Even if I'm doing the dishes, he'll lay down on the floor, next to my feet at the base of the cabinet door. There have been times when Morgan was asleep and I'd move to go into another room, he would wake up and follow me there. He's like my little shadow. And you know what? Although oftentimes he is in my way, he doesn't even bother me.

Jesus desires that we willfully follow His lead. We are to trust that He knows the path we should take in our lives.

Prayer: Lord, help us to realize that you know what is best for us; help us to follow you wherever you lead. In Jesus' name, amen.

3. Helpless and Dependent

…casting all your care upon Him,
for He cares for you.
(1 Peter 5:7 NKJV)

It was approximately 10:30 pm and Morgan had begun to cough and heave uncontrollably. Later, I found out that he was ill with a "kennel cough", a virus that dogs get from other dogs. He was so sick, I honestly didn't know if he would make it through the night. I watched his little body lay limp, almost lifeless. He was helpless and could do nothing. He was totally dependent upon me to take care of him.

Often, I think I can take care of myself and that I can get along just fine without the help of the Lord, especially when handling small matters. From watching Morgan that night, I was reminded of times when we too can hurt both physically and emotionally. But, no matter what situation we face in life, we can be assured that God is concerned and will take care of us.

Prayer: *Lord,* please help us to realize that we are helpless without you and that we must depend on you in all we do. In Jesus' name, amen.

4. The Crate - A Holding Place

Rest in the LORD, and wait patiently for Him;... **(Psalm 37:7A NKJV)**

My husband and I are using the crate to train Morgan. I was told by his dog trainer that when using this method, not to place him in the crate as a form of punishment. Now, I'll admit that often when Morgan has gotten me upset, I'd put him in there anyway! Sometimes, Morgan would go in calmly, but most of the time, he would go in with reluctance. You see, the crate is a holding place where his movement is restricted. I have placed him in the crate for different reasons, so that I can prepare his food or clean up a spill. If I did spill something and didn't put Morgan away, he would have tried to lick it up immediately, and depending on the spill, he could have gotten seriously injured. He doesn't realize this yet, but whatever it is I'm doing, it is ultimately for his protection.

Sometimes, God puts us in a holding place. While there, regardless of how hard we try we can't do much because we are restricted in one way or another. This crate could represent a number of inconvenient and unfavorable conditions, such as waiting for an answer to prayer, healing from sickness, guidance or direction. I wish that I could say that every time God has had me in a holding place that I remained there willingly and was patient, but I can't. Most times, like Morgan, I gotten angry and upset. But, then I had to remember, and I encourage you as well, that God is in control and that if we're placed in those uncomfortable holding places, it is for our best interest.

Prayer: Lord, help us to rest and wait patiently for you when we're in those uncomfortable places in life. Help us to realize that you are working things out for our good. In Jesus' name, amen.

5. Being Stubborn

Trust in the LORD with all your heart, And lean not on your own understanding; In all your ways acknowledge Him, And He shall direct your paths. Do not be wise in your own eyes;...
(Proverbs 3: 5, 6,7A NKJV)

Morgan was just nine weeks old and so stubborn! When we would go walking, if Morgan decided that he wanted to go in a different direction, he would resist by pulling in the opposite direction. Could you believe that sometimes, he would even stop walking and sit down in one place as if in protest? What Morgan didn't realize was that I was a lot bigger and stronger than he, so that his efforts to pull away were fruitless. Why, he could barely run across the grass in our front yard!

Observing Morgan's behavior, made me realize that you and I are no different. God tries to lead us in one direction and we resist, simply because we want to be in control and do our own thing. And like Morgan, ultimately, this behavior gets us no where. In order to please God, we must yield and do as He asks.

Prayer: Lord, please help us to willingly obey and follow your instructions. In Jesus' name, amen.

6. Love

You shall love the LORD your God With all your heart, with all your soul, And with all your strength.
(Deuteronomy 6:5 NKJV)

I've learned a lot about God's love, simply based on my relationship with my dog. Morgan gives me an open display of his love for me by licking my face and wagging his tail. Morgan makes a point to remain close to me wherever I go. And whenever I return after being away, he gives me the warmest greeting by standing on hind feet and frantically waving his two front paws as if to say, "I'm so glad you're home, I've really missed you a lot!" He makes me feel loved.

God wants us to openly demonstrate our love for Him. How do we do this? We show our love through praise, worship, prayer, obedience, fellowship, and reading His word. God delights in our expression of love for Him.

Prayer: Lord, thank you for your love. Help us to openly and freely express our love for you. In Jesus' name, amen.

7. His Efforts To Please Me

And He who sent Me is with Me. The Father has not left Me alone, for I always do those things that please Him. (John 8:29 NKJV)

I've come to realize that Morgan sincerely wants to please me, of course, not 100% of the time, but most of the time. He soon learned that there were benefits associated with obedience; they are called "treats" a yummy snack for dogs!

Again, in a fresh way, I realized how I should make a practice of seeking to please the Lord in all that I do, all of the time. It is our obedience to His word that brings Him great joy.

Prayer: Lord, help each of us to please you in our actions. In Jesus' name, amen.

8. Being Inconvenienced

Let this mind be in you which was also in Christ Jesus, who, being in the form of God, did not consider it robbery to be equal with God, ... And being found in appearance as a man, He humbled himself and became obedient to the point of death, even death of the cross.
(Philippians 2: 5, 6, 8 NKJV)

The second day that I had Morgan, I had to take him on a long distance trip. My husband was away so I had to do this alone. The day before, I had gone to the pet store and purchased Morgan a traveling case because the trip was going to be a 3 1/2 hour drive to my parent's home.

Now, I'll admit, I am no fun to travel with. In fact, I'd get on your nerves because I always want to stop at to take a restroom break. Well, this trip wouldn't be any different, or so I thought. Morgan was only nine weeks old and was not yet house broken. So, because I didn't want him to "wet" in his new travel case, I found myself catering to Morgan's every need! I remember seeing the sign for the first rest area and wanting to stop, but I didn't, Morgan was sleeping and I didn't want to wake him up. So, if I didn't stop for Morgan that meant that I didn't stop for myself either. You would have thought that he was a baby!

After a couple of hours, Morgan woke up. He had started whining and moving about in his box. So when I saw the second rest area I stopped, but only to allow Morgan to go for a walk and stretch his legs. This rest area was crowded. Morgan was beginning to draw a lot of attention, because he was so cute. Not wanting anyone to steal him, I didn't stay long at all. I quickly put him back into the car and left. And, finally, I could not wait any longer, I had to go! When I approached the third rest area, I left Morgan in the car and rushed into the restroom. All the time

I was in there, I couldn't stop thinking that someone would take him.

Wow, talk about being inconvenienced! The entire trip, I put aside my own comfort to make sure that Morgan's needs were taken care of first. Was this crazy or what? Believe it or not, this reminds me of how Jesus inconvenienced Himself, left heaven and came down to live with man. His purpose… so you and I could know more about the love that God has for us and that our relationship with HIM could be restored.

Prayer: Dear Jesus, thank you for being willing to leave the comfort of heaven to meet our greatest need, the opportunity to have eternal life with You. In Jesus' name, amen.

9. The Watchful Eye

The eyes of the LORD are on the righteous, And His ears are open to their cry. …The righteous cry out, and the LORD hears, And delivers them out of all their troubles.
(Psalm 34: 15, 17 NKJV)

I enjoy watching my puppy when he is playing, eating, or sleeping. I study his behavior, so that I can know how to meet his needs. When Morgan barks in a certain tone, I know that he wants attention. I can tell when he wants to play, when he doesn't want to be bothered, or when he's not feeling well. I know this because I'm constantly watching him. As you know, when you study something or someone, you must be in close proximity. I do this because I care.

God is like that with us, always near, watching over us. God is described as being omniscient – all seeing and all knowing. He constantly knows everything even our thoughts. Why does he unceasingly do this? He does it because He truly cares and wants to meet our every need.

Prayer: Father, thank you for being so attentive to us and for caring enough to help us when in need. In Jesus' name, amen.

10. Never Alone

Have I not commanded you? Be strong and of good courage; do not be afraid, nor be dismayed, for the LORD your God is with you wherever you go. **(Joshua 1: 9 NKJV)**

Morgan likes to quietly play on the floor with his toys. Every now and then, he will stop and look up at me as if to make sure that I was still in his presence. When he does this, I can sense his level of comfort in just knowing that I am near. He feels safe and protected. He knows that all is well and he doesn't have to fear for anything.

I have even noticed that Morgan likes to sleep by my feet. It doesn't matter where I am, in the kitchen, bathroom or at the dining room table. He will come right next to my feet and fall asleep.

Just as Morgan finds comfort when I'm in his presence, we can find comfort in knowing that God is always with us. He is omnipresent, which means that He is everywhere at all times. In His word, He tells us that we don't have to be afraid of anything because He is with us wherever we go. That includes in the operating room, courtroom, and on the job.

Prayer: Father, thank you so very much for never leaving us alone. It is a blessing to know that you are always near. In Jesus' name, amen.

11. The Big Mess

If we confess our sins, He is faithful and just to forgive us our sins and to cleanse us from all unrighteousness. **(I John 1:9)** *For You, Lord, are good, and ready to forgive, And abundant in mercy to all those who call upon You.* **(Psalm 86:5 NKJV)**

Morgan is still in the process of being house trained. Could you believe that he had an accident in the house at least three times yesterday? I was so upset; he hadn't done that before…three times in one day! The first time, I didn't scold him, I thought to myself, okay, and anyone could make a mistake. The second time, I told him that I was disappointed and that I didn't like cleaning up his mess. Mind you, I'm speaking to him as if he is a child that understands my every word.

I was so frustrated, that even though the dog training book stated that I wasn't supposed to do this, I proceeded to immediately place him in his crate for punishment! Honestly, at that point, I didn't care what the dog training manual stated. Later that evening, Morgan used the bathroom in the house for the third time; I had my husband to clean it up. I had had enough!

However, in spite of all of the accidents Morgan had made that day, I still loved him, and that love didn't waiver for one moment. Morgan is very special to me, so even though I was upset at what he had done, I never once stopped loving him.

This was a very powerful lesson for me. This reminded me of God's love for us. We are cherished in His eyes; God actually adores us! We, like Morgan, make big messes too! Some we can control, some we can't. Our messes are comparable to sin and even though we will receive punishment for our sins, He *never* stops loving us, no not for one moment.

Prayer: Dear God, help us to obey you and not make unnecessary messes in our lives. But when we do, help us to come to you for cleansing. In Jesus' name, amen.

12. Being a Parent

If any of you lacks wisdom, let him ask of God, who gives to all liberally and without reproach, and it will be given to him. **(James 1:5 NKJV)**

I can say that I have a new level of respect for all parents. I have always heard people say this, but now I know it to be true, that having a puppy is just like having a baby in the house! I must feed, groom, wash, and walk him in addition to all of my other responsibilities. It takes time out of my already busy day and I expend so much energy. I look forward to my husband coming home from work so he can take Morgan off of my hands. My husband is good about playing or walking him so that I can do something else like prepare dinner. Hey, this makes me wonder if my husband has his own "dinner" agenda!

Just by having a dog, I can tell that being a parent isn't an easy job! Parents have so many responsibilities with raising children. Parents, how do you do it?

I have heard many parents say that they would not be able to do this if it were not for God's help. They have found God to give them wisdom and guidance along the way. After all, children belong to Him!

Prayer: Heavenly Father, we realize that especially in today's times, we need your help to raise children. We ask you for divine wisdom. In Jesus' name, amen.

13. Comfort During Painful Times

Blessed be the God and Father of our Lord Jesus Christ, the Father of mercies and God of all comfort, who comforts us in all our tribulation, that we may be able to comfort those who are in any trouble, with the comfort with which we ourselves are comforted by God.
(2 Corinthians 1: 3, 4 NKJV)

Today was an uncomfortable day for me. Morgan received two vaccinations and was in a lot of pain. Initially, when the doctor gave him the injections, he was fine. But after about 30 seconds, he began to cry out in excruciating pain. He saw me in the room, and he came over as if to let me know that he was hurting. I held him close and softly rubbed his head. I tried to comfort him to let him know that everything was going to be alright. I felt so helpless; he was pitiful.

I don't like seeing my puppy in pain. But, even though I know that there would be pain, I realized that this doctor's visit was needed for his overall good and the pain would be short lived. I allowed Morgan to go through this unpleasant experience because he needed to have those vaccinations.

Our heavenly Father is like that too. He doesn't like it when we hurt. But, just as I had to allow Morgan to get those vaccinations for his physical health, sometimes God will allow us to experience painful situations knowing that in the end, they are beneficial for our spiritual growth and development.

Prayer: Father, we realize that sometimes pain is necessary for our growth. Thank you for being there to provide comfort during those times. In Jesus' name, amen.

14. Staying Close to the Master

I am the vine, you are the branches. He who abides in Me, and I in him, bears much fruit; for without Me you can do nothing. **(John 15: 5 NKJV)**

When I go outside with Morgan, I place a leash on him. He doesn't particularly like wearing the leash, because he wants to roam all over the place. He doesn't realize that he has to wear the leash for his own protection. Once, there was a time, I let him out and his leash slipped out of my hands. Immediately, Morgan ran across the street towards the neighbor's house. Realizing the possible danger of getting hit by a car, I began to chase after him. Of course, he thought I was playing a game and continued to run. When I finally caught Morgan, I scolded and disciplined him. When will he learn not to run away from me? Staying close to me is for his safety.

In the scriptures, Jesus speaks of the importance of staying close to Him. How do we do that? By praying and reading His word. All throughout the Bible, Jesus lets us know that without Him we can do nothing.

Prayer: Father, help us to realize that staying close to you and abiding in your word is for our ultimate good. In Jesus' name, amen.

15. The Price for Disobedience

For whom the LORD loves He chastens... (Hebrews 12: 6A NKJV)

Morgan loves to chew on electrical cords in the house. Every time I catch him I'll tell him to stop and remove the cords. Morgan doesn't realize that he could be seriously injured. As his master, I'm ultimately responsible for his protection and safety. So, when he continues to chew on the cords after I've told him stop, he is disciplined. I must do this in order to obtain desired behavior. Morgan has to realize that there are consequences for not following instructions. Continuing to chew on the cords could result in electrocution. I discipline Morgan because I want to correct behavior that can cause him harm.

You can probably tell by now, that Morgan has a lot of behaviors that need correcting!

Most parents expect their children to obey their rules and if not, they suffer the consequences. Regardless of the type of disciple, whether placed on restrictions or spanked, the underlying motive should be love. Just as parents expect obedience from their children, our heavenly Father expects obedience from us. God's guidelines and rules outlined in the Bible and are for our good. If followed, we will find our lives blessed. If not, we too will be disciplined.

Prayer: Dear God, help us to obey you and know that when we are disobedient, you will chastise us. May we find comfort in knowing that your chastisement is motivated by pure love. In Jesus' name, amen.

16. Labels

Every good gift and every perfect gift is from above, and comes down from the Father of lights, with whom there is no variation or shadow of turning.
(James 1:17 NKJV)

When Morgan was a puppy, I took him to obedience school. In eight weeks, he was supposed to learn some basic commands such as; wait, sit, and come, etc. His class consisted of only two puppies, Morgan and a Chihuahua. After closely observing the dogs, I noticed they had different personalities. The Chihuahua was very quiet and timid, and on the other hand, Morgan was extremely active. Morgan was truly enjoying the training; he loved the other puppy and the trainer. However, it appeared as though the little Chihuahua dreaded the entire learning experience.

After a couple of sessions, the trainer began to make comments that Morgan would be a prime candidate for a dog with Attention Deficit Disorder (ADD). Initially, I laughed thinking she was joking, but then at the next training session, she commented that I should ask my veterinarian for medication that would calm him down. ADD for dogs!

After watching him a while, I began to take her seriously and wondered if something was indeed wrong with Morgan. I discussed this with my husband and he said "there wasn't anything wrong with Morgan and that we were not going to give him any medication." He explained that Morgan was just an extremely active, but happy dog.

I had to remember that Morgan my special gift from God. He was perfect. And I was not going to allow anyone to convince me otherwise!

This reminds me of what happens all too often in society; labels are placed on people for various reasons, it could be for their looks, race, background, or behavior. And if we aren't careful, we will start to believe and act on these labels; much like a self fulfilling prophecy. Do not allow people to label you or those you love. Simply be who God intended for you to be and know that you are beautifully and wonderfully made.

Prayer: Dear God, thank you for making us perfect in your image. In Jesus' name, amen.

17. Giving the Best

If you then, being evil, know how to give good gifts to your children, how much more will your Father who is in heaven give good things to those who ask Him!
(Matthew 7:11 NKJV)

Morgan was still taking training classes to learn various commands. His trainer freely shared tips and suggestions for taking care of our animals. One day we were in a discussion about Morgan's diet and I told her the brand of dog food that I used to feed him. She replied that the particular brand was at the "bottom of the list" as far as proper dog nutrition was concerned. She then recommended several other brand names that were considered much healthier for him.

Immediately after the training session, I went to the pet store to find and purchase one of the brands the trainer had recommended. Even though I had just recently purchased a brand new bag of Morgan's regular dog food, I was willing to purchase the recommended brand, because I wanted only the best for my little dog!

God is that way with us. He wants what is best for us in our lives and He will give us what is best, if we trust Him to do so.

Prayer: Father, thank you for giving us your best when you gave us Jesus, your only son. Help us to give our best to you. In Jesus' name, amen.

18. The Restful Trip

Rest in the Lord, and wait patiently for Him... **(Psalm 37:7A NKJV)**

Morgan loves to ride in the car with me. It is a great way for him to relax, because it is soothing and calming to him. My husband and I were in the midst of a job relocation, and it was arranged that I would move first to set up camp. Honestly, I didn't know what I would be facing or even to expect upon my arrival. I was going to a brand new city in which I was quite unfamiliar.

Again, I learned a valuable lesson from Morgan; as I drove the car that day he snuggled into my arms and went right to sleep. Even though he didn't know where I was taking him or that our lives were going to change in a big way, he simply trusted that I would take care of Him.

This is what God wants from His children, to completely rest and trust in Him. Life experiences and relationships are like trips, often, we don't know where we are going, but God wants us to be reminded that He knows our future and has our lives safely in his hands.

Prayer: Dear God, help us to completely rest in you. In Jesus' name, amen.

19. Worms

A wise man will hear and increase learning, And a man of understanding will attain wise counsel...
(Proverbs 1:5 NKJV)

Morgan likes to eat worms! I noticed that during our morning walks, he would try to eat the earth worms that had surfaced on the sidewalks. After prying open his mouth to remove the worms, I would explain to him that he shouldn't eat worms (again, as if he could understand what I was saying). But, regardless to how often I would scold him, he would continue to try.

Finally, because he refused to listen, it got to the point where I allowed him to eat the worms, get sick, and even vomit! I had heard how sensitive a dog's stomach can be to foreign substances. But, I had to let him get sick and see that eating the worms wasn't a pleasant experience after all, and then hope that he would eventually stop!

Our heavenly Father sometimes allows us to have similar experiences, no, not eating worms; but experiences that can be unpleasant, particularly if we refuse to listen. For example, have you ever wanted something so badly that you would do almost anything for it? You thought about it day and night and wanted it regardless of the cost. Sometimes, when we continue to ask God for something, even after He has said no, He will permit us to have it, even though it may be to our detriment. Why would a loving God allow this? He will do this so that we can learn an important lesson, yes, even if it is the hard way.

Prayer: Dear Lord, help us to be good listeners and learn lessons from reading and hearing your word rather than through negative experiences. In Jesus' name, amen.

20. Patience

> *But let patience have its perfect work, that you may be perfect and complete, lacking nothing.*
> **(James 1:4 NKJV)**

If I were to describe myself with one word, "patience" would not be the one. Many times, I have said that I would not have a child because I just didn't have enough patience. The crying, changing of the diapers and midnight feedings are things I could not imagine myself enduring... that is until Morgan came along. People often say that having a dog was just like having a baby because they need constant care and attention. I totally agree!

Surprisingly, I've have found that I have a lot of patience with Morgan. He does everything you can possibly imagine to provoke my anger, like destroying computer chords, ripping up important papers and being disobedient. Still, in spite of his negative behavior, I find myself being patient with him.

Just imagine if God punished us every time we made a mistake, we would all be destroyed! God is patient with us even when we don't deserve it. I'm thankful that he is longsuffering and kind. Our heavenly Father, just as our earthly parents, doesn't give up or stop loving us just because we test His patience. He continues to work with us to bring out our best.

Prayer: Father, thank you for the great patience you have towards your children. May we also demonstrate patience with others. In Jesus' name, amen.

21. My Delight

The Lord delights in those who fear him, who put their hope in his unfailing love. **(Psalm 147:11, NIV)**

I give Morgan the things that he needs and things I want him to have. I find joy in buying special things because I find delight in him. Yes, he is a dog who is extremely privileged!

May the Lord find delight in us. For those of us who have accepted Jesus as our Lord and Savior, we are privileged as well! There are many benefits because of that relationship. The scripture states, "Then the Lord your God will make you prosperous in all the work of your hands and in the fruit of your womb, the young of your livestock and the crops of your land. The Lord will again delight in you and make you prosperous, just as he delighted in your fathers," "If you obey the Lord your God and keep His commands and decrees that are written in this Book of the Law and turn to the Lord your God with all your heart and with all your soul."

Prayer: Father, may we delight in you as well as be a delight to you by obeying your Word. In Jesus' name, amen.

22. Promises to be Kept

…And you know in all your hearts and in all your souls that not one thing has failed of all the good things which the LORD your God spoke concerning you. All have come to pass for you; not one word of them has failed. **(Joshua 23:14 NKJV)**

Guess what? There are times when Morgan behaves well! When this happens I'll tell him that I will give him a "treat". Now, you probably wouldn't think it would be a big deal if I conveniently forgot about the treat…but, I must say, it would be. Believe it or not, Morgan would remember what I told him. How do I know? Well, whenever I make this statement, he walks over to the pantry door and turns to look at me as if to say, "Okay, where is my treat?" Not only does he remember, but I remember as well. I know I could have made this promise without any intention of keeping it, but I take promises seriously and I want Morgan to know that if I promise to do something, I will keep my word. Yes, even though he is a dog!

Our Heavenly Father is like that. The Bible says that "God is not a man, that He should lie, nor a son of man, that he should change his mind." (Numbers 23:19). We are God's creation and we are to remember that He loves us much more than we can imagine. If God promises that He will do something, we can rest assured that He is faithful and will bring it to pass.

Prayer: Father, thank you for the many promises you offer in your word. They are there for us, if we just believe and receive them. In Jesus' name, amen.

23. Permission to Come Near

..let us draw near to God with a sincere heart in full assurance of faith… **(Hebrews 10:22 NKJV)**

Most mornings, Morgan wakes up before I do. I have noticed that he will lie at the foot of the bed and watch for any sign of movement that would indicate that I'm awake. If I'm not quite ready to get up, I'll pretend to be asleep. But if I don't mind him knowing that I'm awake, I will beckon for him with my hand.

Once he sees my hand movement, he knows that he has permission to come near. This usually means that he will get soft kisses, tummy rubs, and back scratches (pure ecstasy for a dog!)

This reminds me of our Heavenly Father who invites us to come close to Him and dwell in His presence. "You have made known to me the path of life; you will fill me with joy in your presence, with eternal pleasures at your right hand."(Psalm 15:11 NKJV).

When we are in the presence of the Lord, He fills our hearts with joy and peace. We feel the warmth of His love, and it feels great! And while in His presence, we should not only receive His love but also, express our love to Him through sincere worship.

Prayer: Father, may we eagerly seek your presence and let you know how much we love and appreciate you. In Jesus' name, amen.

24. The High Price

For you were bought at a price; therefore glorify God in your body and in your spirit, which are God's.
(1 Corinthians 6:20 NKJV)

Morgan is a Bichon Frise and as you may already suspect, my husband and I paid a pretty penny for him. He is a pedigree and has been listed on two registries. Because we invested so much you can understand why we're very protective of him. Morgan hardly leaves my sight! Morgan was purchased for my sheer enjoyment and companionship.

We are all precious to God. God loved us so much that He paid the ultimate price when he gave

His son, Jesus, to die on a cross for our sins. All of this was done so that our broken relationship with our Heavenly Father could be restored. Since Jesus already paid the price, all we have to do is accept His gift of eternal life. Romans 10:13 states, "Everyone who calls on the name of the Lord will be saved." We are extremely valuable to a loving God and He wants our relationship with Him to be restored.

Prayer: Dear Lord, thank you for loving us so much that you gave your only son, Jesus, to die on our behalf. Help us not to take that for granted, but to receive the gift of life. In Jesus' name, amen.

25. Longing for the Master's Return

In My Father's house are many mansions; if it were not so, I would have told you. I go to prepare a place for you. And if I go and prepare a place for you, I will come again and receive you to Myself; that where I am, there you may be also.
(John 14:2-3 NKJV)

Periodically, my husband and I must travel and will need to make boarding arrangements for Morgan. This is always hard for me because I actually miss him when we are away. I have come to believe that he misses us as well. I usually make a call to check on him and see how he is doing. We usually hear good reports like, "He is fine and playing with the staff." Or, "He is eating his food and receiving extra play time outside of the crate."

Now, I don't really know if all of this is true. I really think the staff tells everyone these positive responses, this just to calm their anxieties or concerns. But, there was one particular time that after we had traveled, I went to pick Morgan up from the kennel and asked, how was he while we were away? This time, the response was different, the staff worker stated that "Morgan had been lonely and that he had missed us."

Hearing that response broke my heart, I didn't want him to be sad. In our opinion, we had not been gone long, but to Morgan, it had been forever. He had longed for our return.

I don't know about you, but as a believer in Christ, I long for His return. When I see and hear of all the chaos happening all around us, crime and war, I'll admit, sometimes, I get afraid and feel alone. So often, I find myself praying that Jesus would come quickly. He promised that He will return and take those who believe in Him to a prepared place.

Morgan is fortunate, he has a special place at our home. Have you recently made a visit to a kennel? All of the dogs want to go home with you, and they bark and jump on the cages hoping to get your attention! Unfortunately, they can't go with you because they don't belong to you.

Similarly, when Jesus returns, He is only going to take those who belong to Him back to the beautiful place that he has prepared for us in heaven. Those who have not given their lives to Him will remain, but it doesn't have to be this way. The scriptures tell us, "He is patient with you, not wanting anyone to perish, but everyone to come to repentance." (2 Peter 3:9B, NIV)

The scriptures continue, "But the subjects of the kingdom, will be thrown outside into the darkness, where there will be weeping and gnashing of teeth." (Matthew 8:12 NKJV) This describes a horrible place known as Hell. But again, it doesn't have to end this way, God has provided a way of escape. It is called salvation.

The Bible tells us, "...that if thou shalt confess with thou mouth the Lord Jesus, and shalt believe in your heart that God hath raised Him from the dead, you will be saved." (Romans 10:9 NKJV)

Friend, if you have not asked Jesus to come into your heart, you can do so by believing that Jesus is God's son, that God raised Him from the dead and that He is now in Heaven. Ask God to forgive you of your sins and to come into your heart. If you do this, you can receive salvation and have eternal life.

You can go home with Jesus.

Prayer: Dear God, please touch the heart of the individual reading this little book, that he or she may give their life to you. And as you have used my experiences with Morgan to show your love for me, may this reader be reminded of your great love in a fresh new way! In Jesus' name, amen.

Printed in the United States
118336LV00002B/1-414/P